THE ULTIMATE
ARIZONA CARDINALS
TRIVIA BOOK

A Collection of Amazing Trivia Quizzes
and Fun Facts for Die-Hard Cards Fans!

Ray Walker

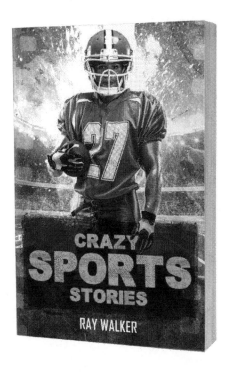

CONTENTS

INTRODUCTION

It is a new era for the Arizona Cardinals, and fans are excited about the Bird Gang. With a star-studded lineup featuring Heisman Trophy winner Kyler Murray and All-Pro wide receiver DeAndre Hopkins, Big Red fanatics have their sights set on an NFL championship.

Cardinals fans are hungry for a Super Bowl contender, and the excitement and enthusiasm surrounding the franchise is at an all-time high. Can this youthful and talented team challenge the Los Angeles Rams, San Francisco 49ers, and Seattle Seahawks for NFC West supremacy? Die-hard fans in Arizona are hopeful that annual trips to the playoffs are just around the corner.

The mission of this book is to celebrate the dynamic history of this well-traveled franchise and the men who have contributed to its success. From Hall of Fame players to legendary coaches, the story of the Cardinals is both heroic and tragic.

The book chronicles the journey of the oldest franchise in the National Football League. From their humble beginning in Chicago to the mediocre days in St. Louis, and the restart in

Arizona, the Cardinals franchise has a unique story that is all its own.

Each chapter consists of 20 quiz questions featuring both multiple-choice and true-false trivia questions, an answer key on a separate page, and a section with 10 interesting "Did You Know?" facts about the team.

Whether you use this book to impress your family and friends with your knowledge of Cardinals history or to compete with other Cards fanatics to see who is truly the team's #1 fan, this book is sure to provide countless hours of entertainment.

CHAPTER 1:

ORIGINS & HISTORY

QUIZ TIME!

1. In which year was the Arizona Cardinals football team founded?

   a. 1893

   b. 1895

   c. 1898

   d. 1899

2. The Cardinals and the Chicago Bears are the only two NFL charter member franchises that have been in operation since the league was founded in 1920.

   a. True

   b. False

3. What was the original name of the Cardinals football franchise?

   a. Racine Normals

   b. Racine Cardinals

   c. Morgan Athletic Club

   d. Racine Street Cardinals

4. Which of the following names was NOT used locally in St. Louis to refer to the Cardinals to avoid confusion with the city's MLB team?

    a. Big Red
    b. Gridbirds
    c. Football Cardinals
    d. The Dirty Birds

5. In what year did the Cardinals become the first NFL franchise to lose 700 games since its inception?

    a. 2010
    b. 2012
    c. 2013
    d. 2015

6. In what year did the Racine Cardinals' name change to the Chicago Cardinals?

    a. 1922
    b. 1925
    c. 1927
    d. 1929

7. Since joining the NFL, how many cities have the Cardinals called home?

    a. 1
    b. 3
    c. 2
    d. 4

8. The Cardinals (5-0) are the only NFL team who have never lost a playoff game at home.

    a. True
    b. False

9. How much was the franchise fee that the Cardinals paid to the NFL in 1920 to become a charter member?

    a. $100
    b. $200
    c. $300
    d. $500

10. The Cardinals had to suspend operations in 1918 because of World War I and a global event. What was the name of this worldwide event?

    a. Cholera pandemic
    b. Measles pandemic
    c. The black death
    d. Spanish flu pandemic

11. The Cardinals and Pittsburgh Steelers merged for the 1944 season due to a player shortage caused by World War II. What was the name of this merged team?

    a. Card-Pitt
    b. Cardinals-Steelers
    c. Steel Cardinals
    d. Pitt-Cards

12. How many points did Cardinals running back Ernie Nevers score in a Thanksgiving Day game in 1929 against the Chicago Bears?

a. 30

b. 36

c. 40

d. 46

13. What was the name of the founder of the Cardinals franchise?

a. Max Winter

b. Chris O'Brien

c. George Halas

d. Charles Bidwell

14. The Cardinals suffered consecutive 0–10 seasons in 1943 and 1944.

a. True

b. False

15. Although the franchise became the Phoenix Cardinals in 1988, the team actually played its home games at a stadium in another city. What city is Sun Devil Stadium located in?

a. Mesa

b. Yuma

c. Tucson

d. Tempe

16. Who scored the lone touchdown for the Cardinals in a 1920 victory against the Chicago Tigers in a "loser leave town" territorial battle?

a. Dwight Sloan

b. Gaynell Tinsley

c. Paddy Driscoll

d. Jimmy Lawrence

17. The Cardinals won their first playoff game in 51 years in 1998. What team did the Cardinals beat to end their postseason win drought?

    a. Chicago Bears
    b. Dallas Cowboys
    c. New York Giants
    d. San Francisco 49ers

18. The Cardinals suspended operations twice, in 1906 and 1918, but has been in continuous operation for how many years in 2020?

    a. 88
    b. 90
    c. 94
    d. 100

19. In 1976, the Cardinals lost a controversial Thanksgiving Day game against the Dallas Cowboys to become the first NFC team to win 10 games without qualifying for the playoffs.

    a. True
    b. False

20. In what year did the American Professional Football Association change its name to the National Football League?

a. 1920

b. 1922

c. 1924

d. 1925

QUIZ ANSWERS

1. C – 1898

2. A – True

3. C – Morgan Athletic Club

4. D – The Dirty Birds

5. B – 2012

6. A – 1922

7. B – 3

8. A – True

9. A – $100

10. D – Spanish flu pandemic

11. A – Card-Pitt

12. C – 40

13. B – Chris O'Brien

14. A – True

15. D – Tempe

16. C – Paddy Driscoll

17. B – Dallas Cowboys

18. D – 100

19. A – True

20. B – 1922

DID YOU KNOW?

1. The Cardinals' first NFL championship in 1925 was marred by controversy because the Pottsville Maroons also claimed to be the league champion. Although the Cardinals lost to Pottsville in their head-to-head matchup, the Maroons were declared ineligible for the title for playing an unauthorized exhibition game in Philadelphia against the University of Notre Dame All-Stars.

2. Although the Green Bay Packers existed before the NFL was established, the Cardinals and the Chicago Bears are the only charter members of the NFL still in existence because the Packers did not join the NFL until 1921.

3. The Cardinals were one of the first NFL teams to use African-American players. Hall of Fame offensive lineman Duke Slater signed with the franchise in 1926 to become the first African-American to play for a current NFL franchise. Slater was the only African-American player in the league for several seasons.

4. The first Cardinal to be elected to the Hall of Fame was fullback Ernie Nevers in 1963. A versatile athlete who could run, pass, and kick, Nevers once scored an NFL-record 40 points in a single game. He also played Major League Baseball for the St. Louis Browns. As a pitcher, he shut out a Detroit Tiger team that included Ty Cobb.

5. The Cardinals' biggest margin of victory in franchise history was a 60-0 win over the Rochester Jeffersons on October 7, 1923. The Cardinals lost three of their final four games to finish in sixth place with an 8-4 record. Rochester struggled to recruit talented players and suspended operations after the 1925 NFL season.

6. Texas Christian University running back Jimmy Lawrence became the first draft pick in franchise history in 1936. However, he only played three mediocre seasons with the Cardinals. He rushed for 357 yards and four touchdowns while catching 27 passes for 253 yards.

7. St. Louis made a rare appearance on *Monday Night Football* in 1983 against the New York Giants in a contest that ended in a tie. The score was knotted 20-20 after four quarters to send the game into overtime. Although the Cardinals dominated the extra quarter, the matchup ended in a tie because placekicker Neil O'Donoghue missed three field goal attempts.

8. The Cardinals' "Million Dollar Backfield" featuring quarterback Paul Christman, halfback Charley Trippi, halfback Elmer Angsman, and fullback Pat Harder led the franchise to the NFL title in 1947. The quartet tallied 282 yards on the ground to defeat the Philadelphia Eagles for their second league championship. Trippi, who starred at Georgia, was the NFL's highest-paid player with a $100,000 contract.

9. The Cardinals are the only team in American professional football history to score exactly four points in a game. In 1923, Chicago recorded a pair of safeties in a 10-4 loss to the Racine Legion.

10. The Chicago Cardinals walloped the Toronto Argonauts in the inaugural NFL-CFL exhibition game in 1959. Although Toronto raced out to an early lead, eight different players scored touchdowns to lead the NFL squad to a 55-26 victory over the Argonauts. The bigger and faster Cardinals used four quarterbacks in the lopsided affair.

CHAPTER 2:

JERSEYS & NUMBERS

QUIZ TIME!

1. The Cardinals introduced a helmet logo in 1960 for their inaugural season in St. Louis. What was this new logo?

   a. Red cardinal

   b. Red cardinal head

   c. Muscular red cardinal

   d. Red cardinal with face mask

2. The Cardinals retired the jersey number of tight end J.V. Cain, who died during training camp in 1979. What was his jersey number?

   a. 80

   b. 82

   c. 84

   d. 88

3. Linebacker Deone Bucannon switched from number 36 to number 20 after his rookie season with the Cardinals.

   a. True

   b. False

4. Which of the following Cardinals' backup quarterbacks was the first player in franchise history to wear number 8?

    a. Paul Collins
    b. Red Cochran
    c. Frank Tripucka
    d. Paul Christman

5. What was the name of the offensive tackle who had his number 77 retired by the Cardinals after dying of a heart attack in 1948 after a game against the Philadelphia Eagles?

    a. Al Klug
    b. Stan Mauldin
    c. Tex Coulter
    d. Jack Carpenter

6. Who is the four-time Pro Bowl halfback who had his number 99 retired by the Cardinals?

    a. Walt Watt
    b. Dwight Sloan
    c. Frank Patrick
    d. Marshall Goldberg

7. Which jersey number did Cardinals defensive lineman Frostee Rucker switch to after wearing number 98 during his first two seasons with the Cardinals?

    a. 92
    b. 90
    c. 95
    d. 96

8. Cedric Oglesby was the third player to wear number 1 in the history of the Cardinals franchise.

   a. True
   b. False

9. Which legendary Cardinals kicker wore number 25 and is the franchise's all-time scoring leader with 1,389 points?

   a. Bill Daddio
   b. Cliff Patton
   c. Jim Bakken
   d. Pat Summerall

10. The Cardinals and Bears are the only two NFL teams with two Hall of Fame players who wore number 13. Which two legendary Cardinals wore the superstitious number?

    a. Larry Wilson and Ernie Nevers
    b. Duke Slater and Aeneas Williams
    c. Ollie Matson and Roger Wehrli
    d. Guy Chamberlin and Don Maynard

11. Which of the following defensive linemen became the first Cardinals player to wear number 94 in 1991?

    a. Eric Swann
    b. Jeff Faulkner
    c. Mike Jones
    d. Michael Bankston

12. The first Cardinals player to wear a number in the 90s was Jerry Lunz in 1925. What number did he wear?

a. 91
b. 95
c. 97
d. 99

13. Besides Night Train Lane, which of the following Cardinals Hall-of-Famers also wore number 81?

a. Paddy Driscoll
b. Dan Dierdorf
c. Jackie Smith
d. Charley Trippi

14. The Cardinals' number 1 was dormant for 73 years from Bill Stein in 1928 to Cedrick Oglesby in 2001.

a. True
b. False

15. Which number did the father and son duo of Terry and Eric Metcalf wear while playing with the Cardinals?

a. 20
b. 21
c. 22
d. 24

16. Which two star running backs for the Cardinals both wore number 23?

a. Larry Centers and John David Crow
b. Elmer Angsman and Stump Mitchell
c. Ollie Matson and Ottis Anderson
d. Johnny Roland and Garrison Hearst

17. Besides number 99, what other jersey numbers did Marshall Goldberg wear with the Cardinals?

    a. 40 and 85
    b. 45 and 87
    c. 42 and 89
    d. 44 and 88

18. Which Cardinals Hall-of-Famer was the third and final player ever to wear the number 8 jersey?

    a. Larry Wilson
    b. Ernie Nevers
    c. Roger Wehrli
    d. Charley Trippi

19. Cardinals quarterback Jim Hart wore number 19 for 18 years.

    a. True
    b. False

20. How many Hall-of-Famers do the Cardinals have who do not have their jersey retired?

    c. 1
    d. 2
    e. 3
    f. 4

QUIZ ANSWERS

1. B – Red cardinal head

2. D – 88

3. A – True

4. C – Frank Tripucka

5. B – Stan Mauldin

6. D – Marshall Goldberg

7. A – 92

8. B – False

9. C – Jim Bakken

10. D – Guy Chamberlin and Don Maynard

11. B – Jeff Faulkner

12. A – 91

13. C – Jackie Smith

14. A – True

15. B – 21

16. D – Johnny Roland and Garrison Hearst

17. C – 42 and 89

18. A – Larry Wilson

19. B – False

20. C – 3

DID YOU KNOW?

The Cardinals have retired five jerseys but only one is for a Hall of Fame player—number 8 for safety Larry Wilson.

In 1988, the Cardinals wore their red jerseys for their first home game, and for the next 18 years in Arizona, the franchise joined other teams in hot climates by wearing their white jerseys at home during the early part of the season to force visiting teams to wear their dark-colored jerseys in the heat.

When the Chicago Cardinals acquired Dick "Night Train" Lane in a trade with the Los Angeles Rams in 1954, he promptly took number 81 from kicker Pat Summerall.

The 1935 Cardinals uniforms featured players' numbers for the first time. The numbers were displayed on the chest and the back of the jersey, which had a crew-neck collar with white trim that extended over the tops of the shoulders.

Number 21 has been worn by the most players in franchise history. As of 2005, a whopping 31 players have worn the number including Earl Ferrell, Richard Fain, and Odie Harris.

The Cardinals debuted alternate black jerseys in 2010

that had white lettering and were paired with white pants. Arizona unveiled an all-black uniform set in 2017 that featured red lettering and black pants for the NFL Color Rush program.

Arizona has four Hall of Fame players—number 1 Paddy Driscoll, number 4 Ernie Nevers, number 62/2 Charley Trippi, and number 35 Aeneas Williams—who have not had their jersey retired by the franchise.

Offensive tackle Fred Gillies is credited with wearing the most jersey numbers in the history of the franchise. Gillies started 51 games for the Chicago Cardinals between 1920 and 1928 while wearing five numbers: 5, 9, 10, 11, and 66. He served as a player-coach in 1928.

In 1989, the Cardinals' road white jerseys added the state flag of Arizona over the top of wide bands of cardinal red striping separated by thin black and white stripes on the sleeve.

Plastic became more common in society after World War II, and the leather helmets that offered virtually no protection were replaced with plastic helmets in 1949. A year later, single face bars were also added to the helmets for even more protection.

CHAPTER 3:

CARDINALS QUARTERBACKS

QUIZ TIME!

1. Which of the following Cardinals quarterbacks was the first player in NFL history to top 4,000 yards passing for three different teams?

   a. Kurt Warner
   b. Josh McCown
   c. Carson Palmer
   d. Boomer Esiason

2. Cardinals Hall of Fame quarterback-halfback Paddy Driscoll was also regarded as the best drop-kicker in the National Football League.

   a. True
   b. False

3. What subject did former Cardinals quarterback Charley Johnson teach as a college professor at New Mexico State University?

a. International business
b. Social science
c. Business administration
d. Chemical engineering

4. What former Cardinals signal-caller was cut after just two starts by the CFL's Toronto Argonauts?

a. Lamar McHan
b. King Hill
c. Ogden Compton
d. Steve Romanik

5. Which of the following Cardinals quarterbacks was one of only two NFL quarterbacks to take every snap for his team in 2001?

a. Jeff Blake
b. Jake Plummer
c. Josh McCown
d. Kent Graham

6. Josh Rosen was a top 10 player in the junior rankings of what sport growing up in California?

a. Golf
b. Chess
c. Tennis
d. Archery

7. Kyler Murray is the only player to ever be drafted in the 1st rounds of both the NFL and MLB Drafts.

a. True
b. False

8. What position did former Cardinals quarterback Logan Thomas switch to after his first two seasons in the NFL?

   a. Punter

   b. Running back

   c. Wide receiver

   d. Tight end

9. How many pass attempts did Ryan Lindley have before throwing his first NFL touchdown pass?

   a. 105

   b. 228

   c. 155

   d. 210

10. Which of the following rookie quarterbacks led the Cardinals to a comeback victory over the Dallas Cowboys on Christmas Day in 2010?

    a. Kevin Koln

    b. Brian Hoyer

    c. John Skelton

    d. Derek Anderson

11. Cardinals quarterback Matt Leinart set an NFL rookie record for most passing yards in a game against the Minnesota Vikings in 2006. How many yards did he throw for to set the record?

    a. 405

    b. 360

    c. 400

    d. 375

12. In his only start for the Cardinals, John Navarre had a terrible game in a loss to Detroit. How many interceptions did he throw against the Lions?

   a. 5
   b. 3
   c. 6
   d. 4

13. Which of the following Cardinals was the NFL's first All-Pro quarterback?

   a. Glenn Dobbs
   b. Paddy Driscoll
   c. Lamar McHan
   d. Paul Christman

14. Jacky Lee is the only player in NFL history to be loaned to another NFL team.

   a. True
   b. False

15. Which of the following quarterbacks was fined over $11,000 for making a crotch chop gesture to Seahawks fans?

   a. Ryan Lindley
   b. Jake Plummer
   c. Drew Stanton
   d. Carson Palmer

16. Which former Cardinals quarterback played for 11 different teams during his NFL career?

a. Jeff Blake

b. Steve Beuerlein

c. Josh McCown

d. Kent Graham

17. The St. Louis Cardinals selected which future Hall of Fame quarterback with the 12th overall pick in the 1964 NFL Draft?

a. John Huarte

b. Joe Namath

c. Tommy Myers

d. Craig Morton

18. Which Cardinals quarterback threw 30 interceptions in 14 games during the 1967 season?

a. Charley Johnson

b. Buddy Humphrey

c. Mike Loyd

d. Jim Hart

19. In 1917, Cardinals Hall-of-Famer Paddy Driscoll debuted in Major League Baseball for the New York Yankees.

a. True

b. False

20. Which of the following quarterbacks is the only person to be named Most Valuable Player of the Sun Bowl in back-to-back years?

a. John Roach

b. Jacky Lee

c. Charley Johnson

d. Gary Keithley

QUIZ ANSWERS

C – Carson Palmer

A – True

D – Chemical engineering

A – Lamar McHan

B – Jake Plummer

C – Tennis

A – True

D – Tight end

B – 228

C – John Skelton

A – 405

D – 4

B – Paddy Driscoll

A – True

D – Carson Palmer

C – Josh McCown

B – Joe Namath

D – Jim Hart

B – False

    C – Charley Johnson

DID YOU KNOW?

Due to his ineffectiveness as a passer, former Cardinal Rusty Lisch was named the worst player in NFL history in 2011 by sports blog *Deadspin*. He threw only one touchdown pass—a one-yarder—in 115 career attempts with 11 interceptions. In 1984, while playing with the Chicago Bears, Lisch started against the Green Bay Packers because of injuries to the team's other quarterbacks. He played so poorly that he was replaced by Hall of Fame running back Walter Payton and finished his pro football career with a dismal 25.1 passer rating.

Neil Lomax is the only quarterback in college football history to throw seven touchdowns in one quarter. The Portland State product threw seven touchdown passes to help his team steamroll Delaware State, 105-0. He finished his collegiate career with 107 touchdown passes.

The Cardinals drafted University of Texas quarterback Rick McIvor in the 1984 NFL Draft even though the signal-caller started only 14 games in college. He had a short NFL career in which he attempted only four passes with no completions. He worked as a wildlife manager at a 120,000-acre ranch before getting elected sheriff of a Texas county.

The Cardinals drafted East Texas State University dual-threat quarterback Kyle Mackey in the 11th round of the 1984 Draft. He posted a 21-10 record as a starter in college but was a backup quarterback in the NFL. The son of former New York Jets tight end Dee Mackey, he started a game for the Miami Dolphins as a replacement player during the 1987 NFLA players' strike. He finished his career with three touchdown passes and six interceptions.

Cardinals Hall of Fame quarterback-halfback Paddy Driscoll was also an accomplished drop-kicker. He booted a 55-yard field goal in 1924 that stood as an NFL record for 29 years. That same season, he wrote a syndicated newspaper article with tips on the proper fundamentals of drop-kicking.

St. Louis selected quarterback Kelly Stouffer with the 6th overall pick in the 1987 NFL Draft, but the Colorado State standout never played a single game with the franchise. After he sat out his entire rookie season due to a contract dispute, the Cardinals traded Stouffer to the Seattle Seahawks for three draft picks. He finished his short NFL career with seven touchdown passes and 19 interceptions.

A member of the famed "Million Dollar Backfield," quarterback Paul Christman was notorious for fumbling the football. His ball-handling skills were so poor that he once fumbled five times in one game, and he set a record one season for recovering eight of his own fumbles. His brother Mark was the starting third baseman for the Browns, the only St. Louis-based team to win an American League championship.

A 10th round draft choice from Southern Methodist University, Ray Mallouf tossed 20 touchdowns and 16 interceptions in 48 games. He holds the distinction of being the first quarterback in NFL history to achieve a perfect passer rating of 158.3 in a game.

Quarterback George Izo was one of the early casualties of the *Sports Illustrated* cover jinx. He appeared on the magazine's cover a week before the 1959 season-opening game but injured his knee in practice a few days later. He missed the first two games of the season and an urban legend was born.

Although St. Louis drafted Steve Pisarkiewicz with the 19th overall pick in the 1977 NFL Draft, he was the ultimate journeyman quarterback. After playing a few games with the Cardinals and Green Bay Packers, he suited up for the Winnipeg Blue Bombers of the Canadian Football League. Next, he joined the United States Football League's Philadelphia Stars before heading overseas to play for several British teams.

CHAPTER 4:

THE PASS CATCHERS

QUIZ TIME!

1. Who is the Cardinals wide receiver who beat future Cleveland Browns cornerback Denzel Ward in the 100-meter dash in high school?

    a. Rob Moore

    b. David Boston

    c. Andy Isabella

    d. Anquan Boldin

2. Hall of Fame tight end Jackie Smith was also the Cardinals' punter from 1964 to 1966.

    a. True

    b. False

3. Which the following Cardinals tight ends is better known for dropping a potential touchdown pass in the Super Bowl as a member of the Dallas Cowboys?

    a. Leonard Pope

    b. Jackie Smith

c. Chris Gedney

d. Taz Anderson

4. Who is the Cardinals wide receiver who ran the fastest 40-yard dash at the 2015 NFL Scouting Combine?

a. John Brown

b. Walt Powell

c. Michael Floyd

d. J.J. Nelson

5. What former Cardinals end was pistol-whipped during a bank robbery in 1975 while working as a bank executive?

a. Ben Kish

b. Steve Lach

c. Al Coppage

d. Gaynell Tinsley

6. In 1975, former Cardinals receiver Dave Williams was the first player signed by a new NFL expansion franchise. What was the name of this new team?

a. Indianapolis Colts

b. Seattle Seahawks

c. Houston Texans

d. Tampa Bay Buccaneers

7. Who is the Cardinals receiver who was replaced by Ahmad Rashad in both St. Louis and Minnesota?

a. Mel Gray

b. Ron Wilson

c. Preston Watkins

d. John Gilliam

8. Speedy Cardinals receiver Mel Gray caught passes in 121 consecutive games between 1973 and 1982.

    a. True

    b. False

9. Which Cardinals wide receiver caught 16 passes for 256 yards in a 1962 game against the New York Giants?

    a. Glenn Bass

    b. Sonny Randle

    c. Max Boydston

    d. Don Carothers

10. Which of the following wide receivers was released by the Cardinals following a DUI arrest?

    a. Andre Roberts

    b. Early Doucet

    c. Michael Floyd

    d. Steve Breaston

11. Who is the former St. Louis wide receiver who said, "When I put God first in my life, my football career boomed."?

    a. Mel Gray

    b. Pat Tilley

    c. Ahmad Rashad

    d. Dave Williams

12. Which of the following Cardinals rookies tied an NFL record in 1979 with a 106-yard kickoff return for a touchdown against the Dallas Cowboys?

a. Mark Bell

b. Roy Green

c. Dave Stief

d. Jimmy Childs

13. Cardinals receiver Ike Harris was honored by *Black Enterprise* magazine as one of the 75 Most Powerful African Americans in Corporate America.

a. True

b. False

14. Who is the former Cardinals tight end who competed in the 1984 Olympic trials as a decathlete?

a. K.D. Dunn

b. Eddie McGill

c. Jay Novacek

d. Robert Awalt

15. Who is the receiver who set the Cardinals' rookie record for receptions and became the first rookie to lead the team in receptions since 1950?

a. J.T. Smith

b. David Boston

c. Larry Fitzgerald

d. Ricky Proehl

16. Anquan Boldin set an NFL record for most receiving yards by a rookie in his first game. How many receiving yards did he have in that game?

a. 163

b. 217

c. 201

d. 189

17. Which Cardinals receiver scored the inaugural touchdown at University of Phoenix Stadium in 2006?

a. Bryant Johnson

b. LeRon McCoy

c. Todd Watkins

d. Jason McAddley

18. Which of the following Cardinals tight ends made national headlines in 2011 by saving a six-year-old boy from drowning?

a. Ben Patrick

b. Rob Housler

c. Leonard Pope

d. Robert Awalt

19. Larry Fitzgerald has been a minority owner of the Arizona Coyotes of the National Hockey League since 2018.

a. True

b. False

20. Who is the Cardinals receiver who died suddenly while playing golf at the age of 36?

a. Ray Kuffel

b. Don Currivan

c. Saxon Judd

d. John Harrington

QUIZ ANSWERS

1. C – Andy Isabella

2. A – True

3. B – Jackie Smith

4. D – J.J. Nelson

5. C – Al Coppage

6. B – Seattle Seahawks

7. D – John Gilliam

8. A – True

9. B – Sonny Randle

10. C – Michael Floyd

11. B – Pat Tilley

12. B – Roy Green

13. A – True

14. C – Jay Novacek

15. D – Ricky Proehl

16. B – 217

17. A – Bryant Johnson

18. C – Leonard Pope

19. B – False

20. B – Don Currivan

DID YOU KNOW?

Larry Fitzgerald was the second active NFL player to become a minority owner of an NBA team in 2020 when he purchased a minority stake in the National Basketball Association's Phoenix Suns. He joins Aaron Rodgers, who became a minority owner of the Milwaukee Bucks in 2018.

Former Arizona 3rd round draft pick Andre Roberts donated $12,000 to the Kirk Cousins Football Camp in 2014 for the rights to wear number 12, as Cousins switched back to the number 8 that he wore in college.

David Boston possessed immense football talent but never fulfilled his athletic potential due to off-field issues. Besides numerous arrests related to drugs and alcohol, Boston was finally sentenced to jail in 2012 for punching a woman. However, he was given only a six-month sentence after convincing the judge that the four concussions he suffered from playing professional football led to his unpredictable behavior.

During his junior year at San Diego State University, Robert Awalt had surgery to remove a rib and reroute an artery and nerve because of a neurovascular problem. He suffered from thoracic outlet syndrome, a group of disorders that occur when blood vessels or nerves in the space between your collarbone and your first rib are compressed.

Roy Green underwent a successful kidney transplant in 2013 because of kidney disease that was associated with his long-time use of anti-inflammatory pills during his 14-year NFL career. The legendary Cardinals wide receiver hauled in 559 career receptions for 8,965 yards and 66 touchdowns.

Speedy wide receiver Mel Gray earned extra money in the offseason running track with Dallas Cowboys speedster Bob Hayes. However, Cardinals owner Bill Bidwell was concerned that Gray might get injured, so he offered him a job driving a train with little kids at Grant's Farms for $1.25 an hour. Gray, who was earning $400 in less than a minute running track, rejected the job offer.

Despite being named a starter after Anquan Boldin suffered a serious injury in 2008, second-year wide receiver Steve Breaston remained on the sidelines during home games instead of participating in pre-game introductions because he felt he was still a backup.

Bryant Johnson played third fiddle behind Larry Fitzgerald and Anquan Boldin during his time in St. Louis, but still managed to post 210 catches and nine touchdowns. In a 2006 preseason game, he caught a five-yard pass from Kurt Warner that was the first-ever touchdown at University of Phoenix Stadium.

In 2008, Anquan Boldin was involved in one of the

most brutal hits in NFL history. During a game against the New York Jets, Boldin was attempting to catch a long pass when he was hit in the back by the Jets' free safety before taking a vicious helmet-to-helmet shot from strong safety Eric Smith. Both players were knocked unconscious, and Bolden missed three games with a concussion and fractured paranasal sinuses.

The 58th overall pick in the 1990 NFL Draft, Ricky Proehl blossomed quickly and caught 56 passes to set a new Cardinals rookie record for receptions. He also became the first rookie to lead the franchise in receptions since Bob Shaw achieved the feat in 1950.

CHAPTER 5:

RUNNING WILD

QUIZ TIME!

Who is the Cardinals player who became the first player in NFL history to average at least 30 yards per kick return and 10 yards per punt return in the same season?

a. Reggie Swinton
b. Terry Metcalf
c. Steve Breaston
d. Eric Metcalf

Ernie Nevers threw a touchdown pass, ran for a touchdown, and kicked a field goal as the Chicago Cardinals shut out the Providence Steam Roller in the first night game in NFL history in 1929.

a. True
b. False

Who is the former Cardinals running back who holds the record for being the oldest player with 100+ yards rushing in an NFL game?

a. Elmer Angsman
b. Ottis Anderson
c. John David Crow
d. MacArthur Lane

Which Cardinals player shared 1952 Rookie of the Year honors with San Francisco 49ers halfback Hugh McElhenny?

a. Billy Cross
b. Johnny Karras
c. Ollie Matson
d. Johnny Olszewski

Which of the following running backs was forced to leave college because of theft, but returned and eventually had his jersey number retired?

a. Wayne Morris
b. Johnny Roland
c. Reggie Harrison
d. Willis Crenshaw

As of 2020, Charley Trippi was the oldest living member of the Pro Football Hall of Fame?

a. True
b. False

Ottis Anderson sparkled in his NFL debut and just missed breaking Alan Ameche's all-time record for rushing yardage in his first game in the NFL. How many yards did he gain in his first NFL game?

a. 178
b. 187
c. 193
d. 202

Who is the Cardinals running back who played 12 games for the San Jose State University basketball team after most team members quit the program?

a. Stump Mitchell
b. Andre Ellington
c. Tim Hightower
d. Johnny Johnson

Which of the following Cardinals players became the first running back to catch more than 100 passes in a single season?

a. Thomas Jones
b. Larry Centers
c. J.J. Arrington
d. Terry Metcalf

Garrett Hearst became the first player in NFL history to play professional football again after suffering a major injury. What condition did he have?

a. Avascular necrosis
b. Prostate cancer
c. Sports hernia
d. Colon cancer

Ernie Nevers played Major League Baseball with the St. Louis Browns and surrendered two home runs to Babe Ruth during the 1927 season.

a. True
b. False

Which former Cardinal became the only coach to work with the two all-time leading NFL rushers, Walter Payton and Emmitt Smith?

a. Larry Stegent
b. Thomas Jones
c. Johnny Roland
d. Ottis Anderson

Who is the Cardinals' 1993 4th round draft pick who won the 1992 Harlon Hill Trophy as the most valuable player in NCAA Division II?

a. Leeland McElroy
b. Anthony Thompson
c. Ivory Lee Brown
d. Ronald Moore

Frank Sanders, the Cardinals' 1995 2nd round pick, led the NFC in receptions in 1998. How many catches did he have that season?

a. 82
b. 89
c. 95
d. 98

What type of incident caused Fresno State running back Michael Pittman to drop into the 4th round of the 1998 NFL Draft?

a. Domestic violence
b. Drug possession
c. Sexual assault
d. Armed robbery

Who is the Cardinals running back who was named the MVP of the All-Army football team in 1953 after missing the NFL season while serving in the U.S. Army?

a. Billy Stone
b. Ollie Matson
c. Mal Hammack
d. Johnny Olszewski

J.J. Arrington finished 5th in the Heisman Trophy balloting in 2005 after a record-setting career at the University of California.

a. True
b. False

Thomas Jones played three injury-prone seasons with the Cardinals but rebounded to become the 25th player in NFL history to achieve what milestone?

a. 5,000 carries
b. 100 touchdowns
c. 1,000 receptions

d. 10,000 rushing yards

Who is the only Cardinals rookie running back ever to have scored a touchdown in each of his first two games with the franchise?

a. Tim Hightower
b. Ollie Matson
c. Garrison Hearst
d. Terry Metcalf

Which future Cardinals running back was the second leading rusher in NCAA Division I-A behind 1980 Heisman Trophy winner George Rogers as a senior at The Citadel?

a. Theotis Brown
b. Earl Ferrell
c. Stump Mitchell
d. Ottis Anderson

QUIZ ANSWERS

1. B – Terry Metcalf

2. A – True

3. D – MacArthur Lane

4. C – Ollie Matson

5. B – Johnny Roland

6. A – True

7. C – 193

8. D – Johnny Johnson

9. B – Larry Centers

10. A – Avascular necrosis

11. A – True

12. C – Johnny Roland

13. D – Ronald Moore

14. B – 89

15. A – Domestic violence

16. B – Ollie Matson

17. B – False

18. D – 10,000 rushing yards

19. A – Tim Hightower

20. C – Stump Mitchell

DID YOU KNOW?

1. Terry Metcalf was a dynamic running back for the Cardinals who also excelled at returning punts and kickoffs. He set an NFL record with 2,462 combined yards in 1975 before the league instituted a 16-game schedule and was the first player in NFL history to average at least 10 yards per punt return and 30 yards per kick return in the same season.

2. During the 1978 season, running back MacArthur Lane accomplished an amazing feat by rushing for 144 yards at the age of 36 years and 199 days. He established a record for the oldest player with 100+ yards rushing in an NFL game that has yet to be broken.

3. Hall of Fame running back Ollie Matson was also a world-class sprinter who competed at the 1952 Summer Olympics held in Helsinki, Finland. He won a bronze medal in the 400-meter race and a silver medal with the United States 4×400-meter relay team.

4. A 2nd round pick of the Cardinals in 1979, Theotis Brown was a standout running back at UCLA who ran for 274 yards against Oregon in 1978. However, Brown suffered a heart attack at the age of 27 when a blood clot formed and blocked three major branches of his coronary artery. He was forced to retire after playing six years in the NFL and rushing for 2,046 yards and 30 touchdowns.

5. Although Charley Trippi is known for signing a $100,000 contract with the Cardinals in 1945 to become the highest-paid player in the NFL, his longevity off the field has been even more impressive. Trippi, who will turn 99 years old in 2020, is the oldest living member of the Pro Football Hall of Fame and one of the oldest living former American football players.

6. Ottis Anderson was a record-setting collegiate and NFL running back who was the third player in NFL history to score rushing touchdowns in two Super Bowls and win a Super Bowl MVP award. He also was a trusted ball carrier who turned the ball over just three times in 739 touches with the New York Giants after spending seven-plus seasons with the Cardinals.

7. Arizona almost made a huge draft day blunder in the 2015 NFL Draft when the Cardinals' brass intended to select Nebraska running back Ameer Abdullah with the 55th pick in the 2nd round. However, the Detroit Lions drafted Abdullah with the 54th pick and forced Arizona to draft Northern Iowa running back David Johnson with the 86th pick in the 3rd round. Johnson has tallied 48 touchdowns heading into the 2020 season, while Abdullah has only 10 touchdowns.

8. In a span of five days in 1929, Ernie Nevers scored all 59 points as the Cardinals captured wins over the Dayton Triangles (19-0) and the Chicago Bears (40-6). He scored a total of nine touchdowns and five extra points in the two

games and set an NFL record for most points scored in a single game with 40 against the Bears.

9. Ivory Lee Brown was one of the top high school running backs in the nation in 1986 and was drafted by the Cardinals in the 7th round. Although he started only five games for the Cardinals, he did win the 1972 World League of American Football rushing title with the San Antonio Riders. Brown's nephew is future Hall of Fame running back Adrian Peterson.

10. Former Cardinals running back Reggie Harrison, who won a Super Bowl ring with the Pittsburgh Steelers, changed his name in 2020 to Kamal Ali Salaam-El to celebrate his Moorish background.

CHAPTER 6:

IN THE TRENCHES

QUIZ TIME!

1. How many minutes per game did Cardinals center-linebacker Ki Aldrich average during his NFL career?

    a. 40

    b. 45

    c. 50

    d. 55

2. Duke Slater joined the NFL in 1922 and became the first black lineman in league history.

    a. True

    b. False

3. Cardinals offensive lineman Ray Apolskis died of a heart attack in 1960. How old was Apolskis at the time of his death?

    a. 39

    b. 40

    c. 43

    d. 46

4. Which of the following Cardinals offensive linemen did not allow a sack for two consecutive seasons?

   a. Tom Banks
   b. Tom Brahaney
   c. Conrad Dobler
   d. Dan Dierdorf

5. Who is the Chicago Cardinals' two-way lineman who intercepted 11 passes from 1946-49?

   a. Bob Cowan
   b. Bill Fischer
   c. Vince Banonis
   d. Hamilton Nichols

6. How many consecutive games did Glen Ray Hines play in with the Cardinals from 1966 to 1973?

   a. 105
   b. 110
   c. 115
   d. 135

7. Tom Banks was named to the 50th Anniversary Senior Bowl All-Time Team in 1999.

   a. True
   b. False

8. Which Cardinals offensive lineman was declared "Pro Football's Dirtiest Player" on the cover of *Sports Illustrated*?

   a. Joe Bostic
   b. Conrad Dobler

c. Greg Kindle

d. Fred Sturt

9. How many knee replacement surgeries did Cardinals offensive lineman Conrad Dobler undergo?

   a. 6

   b. 7

   c. 8

   d. 9

10. Who is the Cardinals center who anchored the offensive line for Oklahoma's record-setting wishbone offense in 1971?

    a. Dan Peiffer

    b. Dick Kasperek

    c. Tom Brahaney

    d. Wayne Mulligan

11. Which offensive tackle played his entire career with the Cardinals except for one season with the USFL's Memphis Showboats?

    a. Brad Oates

    b. Luis Sharpe

    c. Tootie Robbins

    d. George Collins

12. What type of career did Cardinals offensive lineman Doug Dawson pursue when his pro football career ended?

    a. Bank executive

    b. Motivational speaker

c. Real estate broker

d. Wealth management advisor

13. Joe Bostic played 10 seasons on the offensive line for the St. Louis Cardinals. His younger brother Jeff played for the Washington Redskins.

a. True

b. False

14. What position did Ray Brown play at the University of Memphis before being converted to an offensive lineman at Arkansas State University?

a. Safety

b. Linebacker

c. Running back

d. Tight end

15. Which former Cardinal became a documentary producer who won an Academy Award for Best Documentary Feature?

a. Ernest Dye

b. Ed Cunningham

c. Ben Coleman

d. Jeff Christy

16. Who is the legendary Cardinals offensive lineman who became the second African-American judge in Chicago history?

a. Ray Brown

b. Mike Taylor

c. Duke Slater

d. Lomas Brown

17. What was the name of the franchise that offensive lineman Ben Coleman operated while playing for the Jacksonville Jaguars?

a. McDonald's

b. 7-Eleven

c. Yellow Cab Pizza

d. Cold Stone Creamery

18. Which of the following offensive linemen was involved in a tragic car accident in 1999 that ended his pro football career?

a. Ernest Dye

b. James Dexter

c. L.J. Shelton

d. Anthony Clement

19. Former Cardinals offensive lineman Todd Peat's son, Andrus, was drafted 3rd overall by Arizona in the 2015 NFL Draft.

a. True

b. False

20. Former Cardinals offensive lineman Leonard Davis plays bass in a heavy metal band with two former teammates. What is the name of the band?

a. Miscellaneous

b. Deep Trenches

c. Free Reign

d. Deep Edge

QUIZ ANSWERS

1. C – 50

2. A – True

3. B – 40

4. D – Dan Dierdorf

5. C – Vince Banonis

6. C – 115

7. A – True

8. B – Conrad Dobler

9. D – 9

10. C – Tom Brahaney

11. B – Luis Sharpe

12. D – Wealth management advisor

13. A – True

14. C – Running back

15. B – Ed Cunningham

16. C – Duke Slater

17. D – Cold Stone Creamery

18. A – Ernest Dye

19. B – False

20. C – Free Reign

DID YOU KNOW?

1. A 5th round selection in the 2017 NFL Draft, Cardinals offensive tackle Will Holden suffered culture shock when he arrived at Vanderbilt University in 2011. A resident of a small Florida town with a population of 6,908, Holden was in awe at the size of Vanderbilt. The school had 6,796 undergraduate students, which nearly equaled the population of his entire hometown.

2. The only 1st round draft pick in 2015 to be inactive the entire season, D.J. Humphries, played in only 27 games during his first four seasons in the NFL due to injuries. However, the former five-star recruit played in all 16 games in 2019, and the Cardinals rewarded him with a three-year, $45 million contract extension.

3. Brandon Keith was a massive 6-foot-5, 338-pound offensive tackle who was the biggest player to ever play at Northern Iowa. He became the first player from the school to be drafted by the Cardinals, which selected three draft picks from schools outside Division I-A in 2008, the first time that has occurred since the draft went to seven rounds in 1994.

4. Bryan Robinson was a productive defensive tackle who played in Super Bowl XLIII with the Cardinals. He was active in the community throughout his NFL career and has worked with the Special Olympics, made frequent

school visits, and has distributed turkeys on Thanksgiving to low-income residents. He died of natural causes in a Wisconsin motel room in 2016 at the age of 41.

5. Cardinals center Mason Cole has already established himself as an "iron man" on the gridiron. He became only the fourth rookie in team history to start every game during his first NFL season, and he started 120 consecutive games dating back to his freshman season in high school. However, he was relegated to a backup role in 2019 due to the Cardinals' desire for a veteran center to aid in the development of quarterback Kyler Murray.

6. Veteran offensive tackle Marcus Gilbert's father is a retired Secret Service agent who has protected two U.S. presidents, Bill Clinton and Barak Obama. During a visit to the White House in 2008 to celebrate the Florida Gators' national championship, Gilbert received a special shout-out from President Obama.

7. Guard Justin Pugh has been both versatile and consistent during his first six seasons in the NFL. Besides starting 86 games in his natural position, he has also made starts at every position on the offensive line except for center.

8. A converted defensive lineman who was the 225th overall pick in the 2012 NFL Draft, J.R. Sweezy has developed into a solid offensive lineman who has started 94 NFL games despite missing the entire 2016 season due to injury. He joined the Cardinals on a two-year deal in 2019 and started all 16 games during his first season in Arizona.

9. The 5th overall pick in the 2007 NFL Draft, Levi Brown has prepared himself for a successful career off the football field. He earned two Bachelor of Science degrees at Penn State, in labor and industrial relations and psychology, and began his pursuit of a master's degree before his pro football career began. Brown earned his master's degree in professional studies for human resources and employment relations in 2016.

10. A West Point graduate who studied physics and nuclear engineering, Brett Toth was the first person to represent Army at the Senior Bowl in 2018. He is also a second lieutenant in the United States Army.

CHAPTER 7:

THE BACK SEVEN

QUIZ TIME!

1. Which defensive back set an NFL record with 14 interceptions in his rookie season?

   a. Ken Greene
   b. Norm Thompson
   c. Lionel Washington
   d. Dick "Night Train" Lane

2. Washington State safety Deone Bucannon was considered one of the top safety prospects in the 2014 NFL Draft.

   a. True
   b. False

3. Which of the following cornerbacks selected in the 2019 NFL Draft posted his first interception against the Tampa Bay Buccaneers?

   a. Cedric Mack
   b. Jimmy Hill
   c. Byron Murphy
   d. Robert Massey

4. In the 1999 season, which blitzing Cardinals cornerback delivered a vicious hit to San Francisco 49ers quarterback Steve Young that effectively ended his career?

   a. Antrel Rolle
   b. Aeneas Williams
   c. Tom Knight
   d. Corey Chavous

5. Which former Cardinals safety was a Heisman Trophy finalist as a college sophomore before getting booted off the team the following season?

   a. Eric Green
   b. Tyrann Mathieu
   c. Duane Starks
   d. Mickey Washington

6. What course did Cardinals cornerback Justin Bethel plan to study in college before getting interested in playing football?

   a. Psychology
   b. World history
   c. Interior design
   d. Culinary arts

7. Patrick Peterson was invited to the Pro Bowl in each of his first eight seasons in the NFL.

   a. True
   b. False

8. Who is the talented Cardinals linebacker whose career was derailed by substance abuse?

a. Ken Harvey
b. Tim Kearney
c. James Darling
d. Daryl Washington

9. How many times did Dominique Rodgers-Cromartie switch jersey numbers during his NFL career?

   a. 3
   b. 4
   c. 5
   d. 6

10. Antrel Rolle became the highest-paid safety in NFL history in 2010 when he inked a five-year contract with the New York Giants. How much was his contract worth?

    a. $30 million
    b. $35 million
    c. $37 million
    d. $39 million

11. Which Cardinals cornerback was described by Hall of Fame quarterback Roger Staubach as the best cornerback he ever played against?

    a. Roger Wehrli
    b. Jimmy Burson
    c. Pat Fischer
    d. Robert Massey

12. Karlos Dansby became the highest-paid inside linebacker in NFL history in 2010 when he signed with the Miami Dolphins. How much was his record-setting contract?

a. $43 million

b. $45 million

c. $47 million

d. $49 million

13. Cardinals Hall of Fame defensive back Larry Wilson once recorded an interception in a game with casts on both of his broken wrists.

a. True

b. False

14. Who is the former Cardinals cornerback who was killed in a shootout at the age of 39?

a. Lance Brown

b. Carl Allen

c. Ronnie Bradford

d. Michael Brim

15. How many consecutive seasons did Antrel Rolle play in the NFL without missing a game due to an injury?

a. 10

b. 11

c. 12

d. 13

16. How fast did University of Missouri speedy cornerback Roger Wehrli run the 40-yard dash in 1969 to improve his draft stock?

a. 4.4

b. 4.5

c. 4.6

d. 4.7

17. Which Cardinals rookie defensive back returned a punt 89 yards for a touchdown in his first NFL game?

    a. Patrick Peterson

    b. Bryant McFadden

    c. Roger Wehrli

    d. Antonio Cromartie

18. How many career interceptions did Dick "Night Train" Lane have when he retired?

    a. 59

    b. 65

    c. 68

    d. 74

19. Dominique Rodgers-Cromartie was born with a non-functioning kidney that was removed when he was eight years old.

    a. True

    b. False

20. How many defensive touchdowns did Aeneas Williams score during his Hall of Fame career?

    a. 10

    b. 11

    c. 12

    d. 13

QUIZ ANSWERS

1. D – Dick "Night Train" Lane

2. A – True

3. C – Byron Murphy

4. B – Aeneas Williams

5. B – Tyrann Mathieu

6. D – Culinary arts

7. A – True

8. D – Daryl Washington

9. C – 5

10. C – $37 million

11. A – Roger Wehrli

12. A – $43 million

13. A – True

14. D – Michael Brim

15. A – 10

16. B – 4.5

17. A – Patrick Peterson

18. C – 68

19. A – True

20. C – 12

DID YOU KNOW?

1. Cornerback Lionel Washington played 15 seasons in the NFL and has parlayed his football experience into a successful coaching career. He has coached defensive backs in both the NFL and the United Football League and served as a defensive coordinator at the collegiate level. His son, Deron, was drafted by the Detroit Pistons in the 2008 NBA Draft and has played overseas for more than a decade.

2. The 5ᵗʰ overall pick in the 1981 NFL Draft, E.J. Junior was a two-time Pro Bowl selection while playing with the St. Louis/Phoenix Cardinals. He became an ordained minister after retiring from the NFL and was elected to the College Football Hall of Fame in 2020.

3. Night Train Lane was an elite athlete whose life got off to a rough start after the three-month-old was left in a dumpster by his parents. Dissatisfied with his job at a factory, he became one of the few players to walk onto an NFL practice field off the street and make the team. He was also so adept at making "clothesline" tackles, which was later banned. His teammates called it the "Night Train Necktie."

4. Ken Greene was the first Washington State University player selected in the 1ˢᵗ round in 13 years when the Cardinals drafted him in 1978. He participated in the

reality show *Amazing Race* with his estranged wife in 2008 in the hope of salvaging his marriage after his infidelity tore their marriage apart. The couple finished second in the competition but decided to give their marriage another try.

5. Cardinals cornerback Norm Thompson never huddled up on defense with his teammates. He felt it was too tiring to go back to the huddle every play and then cover a guy downfield since he knew all the defensive hand signals that came from the sidelines. Because he was the first free agent in NFL history to sign with another team, he was blackballed by the league after retiring and was not able to pursue scouting and coaching opportunities with any NFL team.

6. Bob Atkins was an exceptional athlete who was known for his speed and bone-crunching hits. He worked several years at the Professional United Leadership League (PULL), serving as a big brother and counselor for inner-city teens.

7. Although Pat Fischer was a smallish cornerback at only 5 feet 9 inches, he made a big impact on the football field at the expense of opposing players. During his 17-year career, he became known as one of the NFL's most vicious tacklers. Due to his size, he perfected tackling at angles where he would have the most leverage and avoid injury.

8. Fred Glick's six-year NFL career was cut short by back surgery at the age of 28. He pursued coaching opportunities

in both the collegiate and professional ranks before being named the head coach of the Canadian Football League's Ottawa Rough Riders.

9. Lindon Crow, who began his NFL career with the Cardinals, was a three-time Pro Bowl selection who racked up 41 career interceptions. Playing for the Giants in the 1958 NFL championship, which was the first game to go to sudden-death overtime, he picked off three passes.

10. Travis LaBoy spent only one season in Arizona due to a torn biceps injury after signing a five-year, $22 million contract with $7.5 million guaranteed in 2008. He started the Travis LaBoy Foundation for Supporting Autistic Causes and Kids (S.A.C.K.), which supports a combination of educational, recreational, and physical activities designed to support children with autism and families of children with autism.

CHAPTER 8:

ODDS & ENDS & AWARDS

QUIZ TIME!

1. Who is the defensive tackle who was a consultant and board member for the National Rifle Association after retiring from pro football?

    a. Greg Lens
    b. Dave Butz
    c. Bonnie Sloan
    d. Steve George

2. Despite weighing only 143 pounds, future Cardinals Hall of Fame quarterback-halfback Paddy Driscoll was a standout athlete at Northwestern University.

    a. True
    b. False

3. What company did former Cardinal Stafford Mays work for as an executive after his football career ended?

    a. Sears
    b. Wal-Mart

c. Microsoft

d. Olive Garden

4. Which of the following Cardinals once led a marriage ministry with his wife and worked as a real estate agent in Florida?

a. Rush Brown

b. Grant Hudson

c. Mark Duda

d. David Galloway

5. Former Cardinal Mark Duda played five years in the NFL with the St. Louis Cardinals. At what college did he serve as head football coach?

a. Hocking College

b. Lackawanna College

c. Monroe College

d. Bethel University

6. Who is the Cardinals player who worked as a fitness trainer for space tourists?

a. Ken Harvey

b. Wayne Davis

c. Anthony Bell

d. Ilia Jarostchuk

7. What former Cardinal never attended college and was earning $5 an hour playing semi-pro football?

a. Chad Eaton

b. Colin Scotts

c. Eric Swann

d. Rod Saddler

8. Curtis Greer was a top pass rusher for the Cardinals who was among the players who crossed the picket line during the 1987 NFL players' strike.

a. True

b. False

9. What kind of injury ended the pro football career of linebacker Jamir Miller?

a. Spinal cord

b. Broken leg

c. Concussions

d. Achilles tendon

10. What was the name of the United States Basketball League team that Simeon Rice played with during his second NFL season with the Cardinals?

a. Gold Coast Stingrays

b. Philadelphia Power

c. New Jersey Jammers

d. Connecticut Colonials

11. Which of the following Cardinals defensive ends was a member of the Society of Innocents, a senior honorary society at the University of Nebraska?

a. Tom Burke

b. Calvin Pace

c. Kyle Vanden Bosch

d. Andre Wadsworth

12. What was the name of the Cardinals defensive end who removed Miami Dolphins lineman Richie Incognito's helmet and swung it at him?

    a. Antonio Smith
    b. Dennis Johnson
    c. Kenny Iwebema
    d. Darnell Dockett

13. What are the three languages that former Cardinals linebacker Sam Acho speaks fluently?

    a. English, Russian, and Igbo
    b. English, Tagalog, and Igbo
    c. English, Chinese, and Igbo
    d. English, Spanish, and Igbo

14. Former Cardinals pass rusher Simeon Rice was the fastest player in NFL history to achieve 100 career sacks.

    a. True
    b. False

15. The Cardinals hired the first female coach in the history of the NFL. Who is she?

    a. Katie Sowers
    b. Heather Marini
    c. Jennifer Welter
    d. Callie Brownson

16. The Arizona Cardinals hold the longest championship drought in major U.S. sports history. When was the last time the Cardinals won an NFL championship?

a. 1947
b. 1948
c. 1949
d. 1950

17. In the mid-1920s, the NFL began a color ban that eliminated all African-American players except one. What was the name of the only black player allowed to play in the league?

a. Fritz Pollard
b. Harold Bradley Sr.
c. Bobby Marshall
d. Duke Slater

18. Who is the Cardinals player who earned an MBA from the Thunderbird School of Global Management?

a. Greg Toler
b. Sam Acho
c. Rob Housler
d. John Skelton

19. In 1998, defensive lineman Eric Swann was inducted into the American Football Association's Semi-Pro Football Hall of Fame.

a. True
b. False

20. Which of the following Cardinals set a Colorado state high school record with 57 career sacks?

a. Will Davis
b. Kenny King
c. Calais Campbell
d. Antonio Smith

QUIZ ANSWERS

1. B – Dave Butz

2. A – True

3. C – Microsoft

4. D – David Galloway

5. B – Lackawanna College

6. A – Ken Harvey

7. C – Eric Swann

8. A – True

9. D – Achilles tendon

10. B – Philadelphia Power

11. C – Kyle Vanden Bosch

12. A – Antonio Smith

13. D – English, Spanish, and Igbo

14. B – False

15. C – Jennifer Welter

16. A – 1947

17. D – Duke Slater

18. B – Sam Acho

19. A – True

20. C – Calais Campbell

DID YOU KNOW?

1. Jerraud Powers, who played eight seasons in the NFL, will always be remembered for a strange incident in 2007, when he was playing collegiate football at Auburn. After breaking up a long pass during the fourth quarter against Alabama, he was bitten on his hand by a police dog near the back of the end zone. Apparently, the dog misinterpreted Powers's celebration as an aggressive act.

2. The Cardinals sold Hall-of-Famer Paddy Driscoll to the Chicago Bears in 1926 with the hopes of keeping the talented player from joining the upstart American Football League. Driscoll was offered a big contract from the new league that the Cardinals could not match. Thus, he was sold to the Bears and eventually signed a $10,000 deal to remain in the NFL.

3. The Cardinals were moved to the NFC West in 2002 when the NFL realigned into eight divisions with four teams apiece. A member of the NFC East for 32 years, the Cardinals joined the 49ers, Seahawks, and Rams, which significantly reduced the travel distance for their division games.

4. The Cardinals snapped a 13-game losing streak to the Dallas Cowboys in 1997 with a thrilling 25-22 victory in overtime. However, Arizona lost their next six games and finished the season in the cellar of the NFC East with a 4-12 record.

5. Former Cardinals quarterback Carson Palmer has become an advocate for CBD products to ease the aches and pains from playing in the NFL for 15 seasons. Palmer partnered with Level Select, a performance-based CBD sports cream, in 2019 to promote the pain-relieving products. Besides suffering from chronic neck and back pain throughout his football career, Palmer also broke his arm once and tore his ACL twice.

6. Actress Phyllis Smith had many jobs before she struck it big in Hollywood, including being a cheerleader for the St. Louis Cardinals during the days of the St. Louis Big Red Line Cheerleaders. Although she is best known for playing Phyllis Vance in the television series *The Office*, Smith also is a regular on the Netflix series *The OA*.

7. When the Cardinals hosted the San Francisco 49ers in the 2006 season-opening game at the team's new University of Phoenix Stadium, it marked the first time the franchise had played a home game on opening weekend since 1988. The stadium's air-conditioning system made it possible for the Cardinals to play at home early in the season despite the extreme heat conditions.

8. The Cardinals have endured two winless seasons during the history of the franchise, with both woeful seasons coming in back-to-back years. In 1943, the team was outscored by a margin of 238 to 95 under head coach Phil Handler. The following season, the franchise merged with the Pittsburgh Steelers due to the manpower shortage during World War II but still failed to win a game.

9. The Cardinals and the Chicago Bears have the longest rivalry in the NFL, which will celebrate its 100th year in 2020. The two franchises have butted heads a whopping 93 times with the Cardinals posting 28 wins, 59 losses, and 6 ties. The Bears won 7-6 in their very first meeting on November 28, 1920.

10. In 1959, the Cardinals played a pair of "home" games at Metropolitan Stadium in Minneapolis. The franchise was desperate to leave Chicago, and the NFL was interested in having a team in Minnesota. However, the Cardinals relocated to St. Louis the following season, and in 1961, the Minnesota Vikings joined the league.

CHAPTER 9:

NICKNAMES

QUIZ TIME!

1. Which Cardinals franchise owner was called the "Father of Professional Football in Chicago"?

   a. Walter Wolfner

   b. Charles Bidwill

   c. Chris O'Brien

   d. Dr. David Jones

2. Dick "Night Train" Lane was given his nickname because he preferred to ride trains to games instead of flying on airplanes.

   a. True

   b. False

3. Why was the franchise called the "Cardiac Cardinals" during the Don Coryell era?

   a. 4th quarter comebacks

   b. Poor performances

   c. Too many turnovers

   d. Nail-biting games

4. Ernie Nevers was considered one of the best players in the NFL in the late 1920s and early 1930s. What was his nickname?

   a. Baby Bear
   b. Grizzly
   c. Big Dog
   d. Big Papi

5. Charley Trippi was the final piece of the Cardinals' "Million Dollar Backfield" in 1947. How much was the contract that lured him to the Cardinals?

   a. $125,000
   b. $175,000
   c. $150,000
   d. $100,000

6. Safety Tyrann Mathieu was given a unique nickname due to his dyed blonde hair and ball instincts. What name did his teammates give him?

   a. Blonde Beaver
   b. Honey Badger
   c. Yellow Bobcat
   d. The Wolverine

7. Cardinals quarterback Jake Plummer took the nickname "Jake the Snake" because it was the nickname of his childhood idol, NFL quarterback Ken Stabler.

   a. True
   b. False

8. What kind of jersey won Cardinals quarterback Sam Bradford his nickname, "Sammy Sleeves"?

a. Jersey with no sleeves
b. Jersey with tight sleeves
c. Jersey with long sleeves
d. Jersey with short sleeves

9. Roy Green was a speedy defensive back who was converted to a wide receiver by the Cardinals. What was his nickname?

a. The Jet
b. Scud Missile
c. The Missile
d. Jet Stream

10. Offensive tackle Jared Veldheer, a mammoth of a man who stands 6 foot 8 and weighs 320 pounds, was called "Big Serious" by his teammates. What was his other nickname?

a. T-Bone
b. The Hulk
c. Big Easy
d. The Giant

11. What was the name given to the St. Louis Cardinals' high-octane passing offense in the mid-1970s?

a. Cardiac Cardinals
b. Big Red Air Show
c. Air Coryell
d. Big Red Machine

12. Running back Chris Johnson broke Marshall Faulk's record of total yards from scrimmage with 2,509 in 2009. What nickname did this achievement earn him?

    a. CJ-2K
    b. CJY2K
    c. 2K-CJ
    d. CJ2K

13. Running back Edgerrin "Edge" James is a member of the 10,000-yard rushing club and was elected to the Pro Football Hall of Fame in 2020.

    a. True
    b. False

14. What was the nickname that wide receiver John Brown's grandmother gave to him shortly after birth?

    a. Lil John
    b. Smokey
    c. Smokey Joe
    d. John Boy

15. Former Cardinals tight end Troy Niklas was a 6-foot-7 giant who starred at the University of Notre Dame. What was his nickname?

    a. Goliath
    b. Bigfoot
    c. Hercules
    d. Big Daddy

16. Who gave Cardinals left tackle D.J. Humphries his nickname of "knee-deep"?

    a. Marcus Golden
    b. Levi Brown
    c. Bobby Massie
    d. Bruce Arians

17. The Cardinals' undrafted free agent Ironhead Gallon was given his nickname by his father. What was the inspiration for his nickname?

    a. Ironhead Sportster
    b. Ironhead Motor
    c. Ironhead Harley Davidson
    d. Craig "Ironhead" Heyward

18. What is the nickname that wide receiver DeAndre Hopkins's mother gave him because it was his favorite brand of pacifier?

    a. Avent
    b. Nuk
    c. Playtex
    d. Tommee Tippee

19. De'Chavon "Gump" Hayes was given his nickname at elementary school because he had Forrest Gump speed.

    a. True
    b. False

20. What is the nickname of future Cardinals Hall of Fame wide receiver Larry Fitzgerald?

a. Sir Larry
b. Larry Legend
c. Iconic Larry
d. Larry the Great

QUIZ ANSWERS

1. C – Chris O'Brien

2. B – False

3. A – 4th quarter comebacks

4. C – Big Dog

5. D – $100,000

6. B – Honey Badger

7. A – True

8. C – Jersey with long sleeves

9. D – Jet Stream

10. B – The Hulk

11. C – Air Coryell

12. D – CJ2K

13. A – True

14. B – Smokey

15. C – Hercules

16. D – Bruce Arians

17. D – Craig "Ironhead" Heyward

18. B – Nuk

19. A – True

20. B – Larry Legend

DID YOU KNOW?

1. Tom Tupa, who began his NFL career with the Cardinals in 1988, was the first player in league history to score a two-point conversion. In 1994, Tupa executed a perfect fake extra-point attempt against the Cincinnati Bengals as a member of the Cleveland Browns. He was given the nickname "Two-Point Tupa" after scoring three two-point conversions that season.

2. A 6-foot-8 tight end with soft hands, Leonard "Champ" Pope played for the Cardinals from 2006 through 2008. He has a charity foundation called C.H.A.M.P. The Creating Hope and Making Progress organization is dedicated to helping and mentoring underprivileged kids.

3. Former Cardinals running back Theotis "Big Foot" Brown played only six seasons in the NFL before his career was ended by a heart attack. He rushed for 2,046 yards and 30 touchdowns for three NFL teams and was also called "Chocolate Thunder" for his love of chocolate and his running style.

4. Although he stood only 5 foot 9, "Stump" Mitchell was one of the best players to ever compete for the Cardinals. He got his nickname from his older friends who he played football with as a child. He finished his 10-year career with the second most all-purpose yards in Cardinals' franchise history and rushed for 4,647 yards and 32 touchdowns.

5. While Chris "Beanie" Wells had a relatively short NFL career, he set a Cardinals single-game record in 2011 with 228 rushing yards against the St. Louis Rams. His nickname came at an early age when his big brother started calling him "Beanpole" because he was too skinny.

6. Norm "Sweets" Thompson is best known for being the first NFL free agent to sign with another team. But he was also a gifted cornerback whom the Cardinals drafted in the 1st round of the 1971 NFL Draft. His teammates called him "Sweets" because he made everything look easy.

7. Cornerback Pat "Mouse" Fischer is regarded as one of the best late-round draft selections in NFL history. Despite being the 232nd player selected in the 1961 NFL Draft, he played in the NFL for an incredible 17 seasons and tallied 56 interceptions. He got his nickname due to his 5-foot-9, 170-pound body.

8. Jim "Bags" Bakken had a long, illustrious 17-year career with the Cardinals. He made seven field goals in one game to set an NFL record, and he finished his pro football career with 282 field goals. He was called "Bags" by his teammates, who felt that his kicks were money in the bank when the game was on the line.

9. Clemson linebacker Isaiah Simmons was the Cardinals' top selection in the 2020 Draft. A speedy, versatile player who took snaps at linebacker, defensive end, cornerback, and safety in college, he won the 2019 Butkus Award as the nation's best linebacker. He was nicknamed "Slimmons"

when he was a freshman at Clemson because he was so skinny.

10. The Cardinals made Sam "Con Man" Bradford the top overall pick in the 2010 NFL Draft. He got his nickname for signing huge free-agent contracts from desperate NFL teams despite the fact he struggled to stay healthy and often played poorly when he was healthy. He earned nearly $130 million during his nine-year career despite boasting a record of 34-48-1 as a starting quarterback.

CHAPTER 10:

ALMA MATERS

QUIZ TIME!

1. Who is the Clemson linebacker who received the 2019 Butkus Award as the nation's best linebacker and was chosen by the Cardinals in the 1st round of the 2020 NFL Draft?

   a. Stephone Anthony

   b. Ben Boulware

   c. Isaiah Simmons

   d. Ed McDaniel

2. In 2013, Larry Fitzgerald's number 1 jersey was retired by the University of Pittsburgh.

   a. True

   b. False

3. Patrick Peterson was an All-American at Louisiana State University who won the Jim Thorpe Award as the nation's best collegiate defensive back. What other major award did he win that same year?

a. Heisman Trophy

b. Chuck Bednarik Award

c. Maxwell Award

d. Bronko Nagurski Trophy

4. What college did Kyler Murray attend before transferring to the University of Oklahoma?

a. Baylor

b. Texas

c. Texas Tech

d. Texas A&M

5. Arizona cornerback Byron Murphy made two interceptions, including a 66-yard pick-six, to win the MVP award at the 2018 Pac-12 Football Championship Game. What college did he play for?

a. Washington

b. Ohio State

c. Oregon State

d. Northwestern

6. Ryan Williams rushed for 1,655 yards and 21 touchdowns as a redshirt freshman to set several school and conference records. What ACC school did he attend?

a. Clemson

b. Pittsburgh

c. Virginia Tech

d. Notre Dame

7. Ryan Lindley threw for 276 yards and two touchdowns to

lead which Mountain West Conference school to a blowout win against Navy in the 2010 Poinsettia Bowl?

a. Boise State

b. San Jose State

c. New Mexico

d. San Diego State

8. In 2011, Alex Okafor was named a First Team All-American as a defensive end by the American Football Coaches Association.

a. True

b. False

9. During his sophomore year, Beanie Wells rushed for 222 yards against rival Michigan. What Big 10 school did Wells lead to victory?

a. Maryland

b. Ohio State

c. Nebraska

d. Minnesota

10. Defensive end Calais Campbell recorded at least three sacks in a single game on three different occasions during the 2006 season. What college powerhouse program did he play for?

a. USC

b. Auburn

c. Miami

d. Penn State

11. Although he often faced double-teams, Darnell Dockett set a new single-season record with 22 tackles for loss for what ACC school?

    a. Louisville
    b. Syracuse
    c. Wake Forest
    d. Florida State

12. Adrian Wilson tallied 144 solo tackles, 11 tackles for a loss, 11 pass deflections, and three interceptions as a two-year starter for what Atlantic Coast Conference school?

    a. Georgia Tech
    b. Pittsburgh
    c. Virginia Tech
    d. North Carolina State

13. Simeon Rice had a dominant junior season and enjoyed a stellar outing against Washington State with five sacks, a blocked field goal, and a fumble recovery. What Big 10 school did he attend?

    a. Illinois
    b. Maryland
    c. Wisconsin
    d. Michigan State

14. Wide receiver Frank Sanders was selected in the 14th round of the 1994 Major League Baseball Draft by the Seattle Mariners but opted to remain playing football at Auburn University.

a. True

b. False

15. Jay Novacek won the Western Athletic Conference decathlon championship and placed fourth in the NCAA championships, earning All-American honors in track at what school?

a. Air Force

b. Wyoming

c. Texas State

d. Utah State

16. Cornerback Leonard Smith was adept at blocking field goals, points after touchdown, and punts while earning all-conference honors at what Southland Conference school?

a. Nicholls State

b. Stephen F. Austin

c. McNeese State

d. Abilene Christian

17. Earl Ferrell was the second player in school history to be selected in the NFL Draft and play in the league after playing college football at what Southern Conference school?

a. Wofford College

b. Western Carolina

c. Samford University

d. East Tennessee State

18. Wide receiver Roy Green was an All-American defensive back and return man at what Great American Conference school?

    a. Arkansas Tech

    b. Oklahoma Baptist

    c. Henderson State

    d. Southern Arkansas

19. Neil Lomax once held 90 NCAA passing records and tossed seven touchdown passes in a single quarter for Portland State University.

    a. True

    b. False

20. In 1997, consensus First Team All-American Andre Wadsworth was named ACC Player of the Year and ACC Defensive Player of the Year for what ACC school?

    a. Notre Dame

    b. Georgia Tech

    c. Virginia Tech

    d. Florida State

QUIZ ANSWERS

1. C – Isaiah Simmons

2. A – True

3. B – Chuck Bednarik Award

4. D – Texas A&M

5. A – Washington

6. C – Virginia Tech

7. D – San Diego State

8. A – True

9. B – Ohio State

10. C – Miami

11. D – Florida State

12. D – North Carolina State

13. A – Illinois

14. A – True

15. B – Wyoming

16. C – McNeese State

17. D – East Tennessee State

18. C – Henderson State

19. A – True

20. D – Florida State

DID YOU KNOW?

1. A 10th round draft pick out of Brigham Young University, Vai Sikahema was the first Tongan ever to play in the National Football League. An elite punt and kickoff return specialist, he was a member of the undefeated 1984 Cougars squad that went a perfect 13-0 to claim the college football's mythical championship.

2. Doug Dawson was the Cardinals' 2nd round pick in the 1984 NFL Draft. The 6-foot-3, 238-pound offensive lineman was a consensus First Team All-American at the University of Texas in 1983 and a member of the Friar Society, the oldest honor society at the school.

3. A versatile defensive lineman who played eight seasons for the Cardinals, David Galloway registered 38 quarterback sacks in 99 NFL games. He served as a team captain for the Florida Gators during his senior year and was named a First Team All-American. He is also a member of the Florida Athletic Hall of Fame as a "Gator Great."

4. Dave Ahrens played in 130 games during a 10-year NFL career that started in 1981 with the St. Louis Cardinals. He was originally a fullback at the University of Wisconsin but was converted to a linebacker. During his senior year, he was selected team captain and was named the Badgers' Most Valuable Player.

5. Curtis Greer was a dominating defensive lineman for the University of Michigan who was a consensus All-American during his final season. He holds the school record with 48 tackles behind the line of scrimmage and was a two-time First Team All-Big Ten Conference for the Wolverines.

6. Quarterback Rusty Lisch struggled mightily in the NFL but enjoyed some success during his time at the University of Notre Dame. He led the Fighting Irish to a win over the University of Miami in his first collegiate start and was under center for Notre Dame for the first three games of the 1977 season before future Hall-of-Famer Joe Montana was named the starter. Lisch started all 10 games in his final season and led the team to seven wins.

7. Calais Campbell played college football at the University of Miami and tallied 19.5 sacks in 36 games. The 6-foot-8 defensive end, who was drafted by the Arizona Cardinals in the 2nd round of the 2008 NFL Draft, also had 39 career tackles for loss.

8. LaRod Stephens-Howling was the starting running back for the University of Pittsburgh during his sophomore season and rushed for 893 yards and nine touchdowns. However, he was replaced by future NFL running back LeSean McCoy. He finished his career with 1,959 yards and 15 touchdowns.

9. Brian Keith was a four-star offensive lineman who attended Northeastern Oklahoma A&M College before

transferring to the University of Oklahoma. But due to a lack of playing time, he transferred to Northern Iowa and helped the Panthers offense rank 11th in the country with 31 points a game. Keith was named a Third Team All-American in 2007 as Northern Iowa finished the regular season with an 11-0 record.

10. Former University of Southern California quarterback Matt Leinart is one of the most decorated players in the history of college football. He guided the Trojans to 37 wins in 39 games and won the 2004 National Championship. During his three seasons at USC, Leinart threw for over 10,000 yards and 99 touchdown passes, and his number 11 jersey was retired.

CHAPTER 11:

IN THE DRAFT ROOM

QUIZ TIME!

1. Since 1980, how many times have the Cardinals had two draft picks in the 1st round?

    a. 3

    b. 4

    c. 5

    d. 6

2. The Cardinals have had a 1st round draft pick in every NFL Draft since 1966.

    a. True

    b. False

3. How many times have the Cardinals held the top overall pick in the NFL Draft?

    a. 2

    b. 3

    c. 4

    d. 5

4. In the 1979 NFL Draft, the Cardinals selected a pair of running backs with their first two picks who combined to gain more than 12,000 yards and 111 touchdowns. Who were these two backfield mates?

    a. Garrison Hearst and Ronald Moore
    b. Anthony Thompson and Larry Centers
    c. Ottis Anderson and Theotis Brown
    d. George Franklin and Terdell Middleton

5. How many Hall of Fame players have the Cardinals drafted in the 1st round?

    a. 4
    b. 5
    c. 6
    d. 7

6. Hall of Fame offensive lineman Dan Dierdorf was selected in which round of the NFL Draft?

    a. 1st
    b. 2nd
    c. 3rd
    d. 4th

7. Who is the placekicker that the Cardinals drafted in the 2nd round of the 1986 NFL Draft who played in only 11 games?

    a. Mike Wood
    b. Jay Feely
    c. Joe Nedney
    d. John Lee

8. The Cardinals have drafted seven players who have been inducted into the Pro Football Hall of Fame.

   a. True
   b. False

9. Charley Trippi was selected 1st overall by the Cardinals in which year's NFL Draft?

   a. 1940
   b. 1942
   c. 1945
   d. 1949

10. Which player was selected highest in his draft class?

    a. Eric Swann
    b. Ernest Dye
    c. David Boston
    d. Leonard Davis

11. Who is the placekicker that the Cardinals selected in the 1st round of the 1978 NFL Draft?

    a. Bob Atha
    b. Sergio Albert
    c. Steve Little
    d. Gerald Warren

12. Hall of Fame defensive back Aeneas Williams was selected in which round of the NFL Draft?

    a. 3rd
    b. 4th
    c. 5th
    d. 6th

13. Which defensive back was drafted with the 325th pick in the 1985 NFL Draft and went on to play in 147 NFL games?

    a. Greg Lee
    b. Dupree Branch
    c. Delrick Brown
    d. Lonnie Young

14. During the 1981 NFL Draft, the Cardinals used eight of their 13 picks on offensive players, including four wide receivers.

    a. True
    b. False

15. Which defensive end was selected with the 3rd overall pick in the 1998 NFL Draft and finished his career with eight sacks in 36 NFL games?

    a. Eric England
    b. Andre Wadsworth
    c. Calvin Pace
    d. Dennis Johnson

16. Andre Ellington was a productive running back for the Cardinals despite being drafted in the late rounds. In what round was he selected?

    a. 5th
    b. 6th
    c. 7th
    d. 8th

17. Kyler Murray was selected 1st overall by the Cardinals in which year's NFL Draft?

    a. 2017
    b. 2018
    c. 2019
    d. 2020

18. The Cardinals selected which three linebackers in the 1st round within a four-year period?

    a. Jeff Leiding, Niko Noga, Tim Lucas
    b. Wayne Dillard, Bob Harris, James Lane
    c. Anthony Bell, Ken Harvey, Eric Hill
    d. Wayne Davis, David Bavaro, Terry Irving

19. Renaldo Hill was a 7th round draft pick who intercepted 19 passes in 141 NFL games.

    a. True
    b. False

20. In the 2001 NFL Draft, the Cardinals took offensive lineman Leonard Davis with the 2nd overall pick. Which Hall of Fame offensive lineman did the team pass on?

    a. Jeff Backus
    b. Maurice Williams
    c. Steve Hutchinson
    d. Kenyatta Walker

QUIZ ANSWERS

1. B – 4

2. A – True

3. C – 4

4. C – Ottis Anderson and Theotis Brown

5. A – 4

6. B – 2nd

7. D – John Lee

8. B – False

9. C – 1945

10. D – Leonard Davis

11. C – Steve Little

12. A – 3rd

13. D – Lonnie Young

14. A – True

15. B – Andre Wadsworth

16. B – 6th

17. C – 2019

18. C – Anthony Bell, Ken Harvey, and Eric Hill

19. A – True

20. C – Steve Hutchinson

DID YOU KNOW?

1. The top overall pick in the 2019 NFL Draft, Kyler Murray rewrote the Cardinals' record book for rookie quarterbacks during his maiden NFL season. He started all 16 games for Arizona and passed for 3,722 yards and 20 touchdowns, while rushing for 544 yards and 4 touchdowns. He also won the 2018 Heisman Trophy and the Associated Press NFL Offensive Rookie of the Year Award.

2. Sometimes it is better to be lucky than good. The Cardinals drafted Northern Iowa running back David Johnson with the 86th pick in the 2015 NFL Draft but really wanted Nebraska running back Ameer Abdullah. The Detroit Lions selected Abdullah one pick ahead of Arizona in the 2nd round. Johnson started his NFL career in grand fashion as he became the first player in NFL history with rushing, receiving, and kick return touchdowns in his first two games. The following season, Johnson posted 2,118 yards from scrimmage to lead the league, while Abdullah has only 1,366 yards career rushing yards heading into the 2020 season.

3. The Cardinals gambled and lost when they took University of Mississippi defensive end Robert Nkemdiche with the 29th pick in the 2016 NFL Draft. A gifted athlete blessed with size, strength, and athleticism, Nkemdiche was projected to be the next Reggie White.

Instead, he was an unmotivated player with little focus and desire to be an elite NFL player. While he recorded 4.5 sacks and nine tackles for a loss in 2018, a knee injury combined with weight problems and off-field issues led the Cardinals to release him in training camp a year later.

4. Although Chad Williams caught 90 passes for 1,337 yards and 11 touchdowns during his senior year at Grambling State University, Arizona was roundly criticized when they drafted the wide receiver in the 3rd round of the 2017 NFL Draft. Williams caught only 20 passes for 202 yards and one touchdown in two seasons with the Cardinals before being released in 2019 during training camp.

5. Arizona struck out again in 2016 with 3rd round pick Brandon Williams. The Cardinals used the 92nd overall pick on the Texas A&M cornerback, who was a five-star recruit who played running back in college for three seasons before switching to defense. Although he started the season opener in his rookie year, he only started two more games the rest of the season. He was primarily a special team player the next two seasons and was on injured reserve for the entire 2019 season.

6. The Cardinals finally struck gold, although with risks, in the 3rd round of the 2013 NFL Draft with LSU defensive back Tyrann Mathieu. The talented safety had a spectacular sophomore season when he was a Heisman Trophy finalist and won the Chuck Bednarik Award as the best defensive player in college football. But he was

dismissed from the team for violating team rules and was later arrested for marijuana possession. Still, he quickly blossomed into one of the top defensive backs in the NFL when he was healthy.

7. Florida Gators offensive tackle D.J. Humphries appeared to be another 1st round blunder for the Cardinals in 2016 after a terrible rookie season in which he was the only 1st round pick who never stepped on the field. But the former five-star recruit regrouped in his second season and started 13 games. Although he was plagued by injuries for the next two seasons, he was rewarded with a three-year, $43 million contract after starting all 16 games in 2019.

8. Andre Ellington appeared to be a rare 6th round gem in 2013 after a promising rookie season when he averaged 5.5 yards a carry and had over 1,000 combined rushing and receiving yards. The Clemson product had over 1,000 rushing and receiving yards again in his second year but averaged only 3.3 yards per carry. His production steadily dropped over the next three seasons.

9. The Cardinals traded up in the 2018 NFL Draft to grab UCLA quarterback Josh Rosen with the 10th overall pick. He was forced into action when starter Sam Bradford was injured and led the team to its only three wins. However, Arizona decided to draft 2018 Heisman Trophy winner Kyler Murray with the top overall pick in the 2019 NFL Draft and shipped Rosen to the Miami Dolphins for draft picks.

10. An injury wiped out 2013 4th round pick Alex Okafor's rookie season, but the defensive end from the University of Texas rebounded in a big way the following season with eight sacks in 12 starts. A non-football injury caused him to miss the Cardinals playoff run in 2015, but he returned the next season before leaving in free agency in 2017.

CHAPTER 12:

THE TRADING POST

QUIZ TIME!

1. The Cardinals traded Ollie Matson to the Los Angeles Rams after the 1958 season in a blockbuster deal. How many players did the Rams send to the Cardinals?

    a. 6
    b. 7
    c. 8
    d. 9

2. Matt Barkley developed into a productive quarterback under Bruce Arians after being traded from the Philadelphia Eagles.

    a. True
    b. False

3. Which quarterback did the Cardinals acquire from the Oakland Raiders for two mid-round draft picks?

    a. Kurt Warner
    b. Brian Hoyer

c. Carson Palmer

d. Blaine Gabbert

4. Which standout pass rusher did the Cardinals get from the New England Patriots for offensive lineman Jonathan Cooper and a 2nd round draft pick?

a. Jabari Issa

b. Chandler Jones

c. Simeon Rice

d. Kyle Vanden Bosch

5. In 1991, the Cardinals made a trade with the Miami Dolphins to acquire which speedy wide receiver?

a. Randal "Thrill" Hill

b. Billy Williams

c. Clyde Duncan

d. Stevie Anderson

6. In 1998, Arizona received three draft picks, wide receiver/kick returner Eric Metcalf, and linebacker Patrick Sapp from the San Diego Chargers for moving back one spot to the 3rd overall pick. What rounds were those draft choices in?

a. 1st, 2nd, and 3rd

b. 1st, 3rd, and 3rd

c. 1st, 2nd, and 4th

d. 1st, 1st, and 2nd

7. What did Arizona trade to the New York Jets to acquire safety Kerry Rhodes, who won the Lloyd Herberg MVP Award that same season?

a. Two 3rd round draft choices

b. Running back Beanie Wells

c. 4th and 7th round draft choices

d. Wide receiver Early Doucet

8. Arizona has completed more trades involving quarterbacks than any other position.

   a. True

   b. False

9. Which lineman did the Cardinals receive from the Detroit Lions in exchange for Dick "Night Train" Lane?

   a. Gerry Perry

   b. Phil Blazer

   c. Bill Jerry

   d. Ken Russell

10. Which Pro Bowl wide receiver did the Cardinals acquire from the New York Jets for running back Ronald Moore and two draft picks?

    a. Herman Moore

    b. Jeff James

    c. Johnnie Morton

    d. Rob Moore

11. In a cost-cutting move, the Cardinals traded offensive tackle Jared Veldheer to the Denver Broncos for a 6th round draft pick. How much money did Arizona save?

    a. $3.8 million

    b. $4.3 million

c. $5.5 million

d. $6.9 million

12. What compensation did Arizona send to the New York Jets for running back Adrian Murrell and a 7th round pick?

a. 1st round draft choice

b. 3rd round draft choice

c. 4th round draft choice

d. 2nd round draft choice

13. Which player did the Cardinals receive from the Kansas City Chiefs in 2013 for fullback Anthony Sherman?

a. Cornerback Sean Smith

b. Cornerback Dunta Robinson

c. Cornerback Javier Arenas

d. Cornerback Brandon Flowers

14. In 2017, the Cardinals acquired future Hall of Fame running back Adrian Peterson for $500,000 cash.

a. True

b. False

15. Arizona received a 2nd round draft pick, the 62nd overall, when they sent quarterback Josh Rosen to the Miami Dolphins. Which player did the Cardinals choose with that pick?

a. Wide receiver Hakeem Butler

b. Wide receiver Andy Isabella

c. Wide receiver Christian Kirk

d. Wide receiver KeeSean Johnson

16. Which cornerback did the Cardinals acquire from the Cleveland Browns in 2018 for a 6th round draft pick?

    a. Jamar Taylor
    b. T.J. Carrie
    c. Juston Burris
    d. Phillip Gaines

17. Which running back did Arizona receive from the Miami Dolphins in 2019 for a 2020 conditional draft pick?

    a. Kalen Ballage
    b. Patrick Laird
    c. Kenyan Drake
    d. Samaje Perine

18. Which cornerback did the Cardinals acquire from the Kansas City Chiefs for a 7th round draft choice in 2016? (Hint: He was selected to the Pro Bowl that year.)

    a. Marcus Cooper
    b. Ron Parker
    c. D.J. White
    d. Steven Nelson

19. Arizona acquired veteran offensive lineman Marcus Gilbert from the Pittsburgh Steelers in 2019 for a 6th round draft choice to anchor one of the NFL's best offensive lines.

    a. True
    b. False

20. What package did Arizona send to the Houston Texans to acquire Pro Bowl wide receiver DeAndre Hopkins?

a. Running back David Johnson, 1st, 2nd
b. Running back David Johnson, 2nd, 2nd
c. Running back David Johnson, 2nd, 3rd
d. Running back David Johnson, 2nd, 4th

QUIZ ANSWERS

1. D – 9

2. A – True

3. C – Carson Palmer

4. B – Chandler Jones

5. A – Randal "Thrill" Hill

6. D – 1st, 1st, and 2nd

7. C – 4th and 7th round draft choices

8. B – False

9. A – Gerry Perry

10. D – Rob Moore

11. D – $6.9 million

12. B – 3rd round draft choice

13. C – Cornerback Javier Arenas

14. B – False

15. B – Wide receiver Andy Isabella

16. A – Jamar Taylor

17. C – Kenyan Drake

18. A – Marcus Cooper

19. B – False

20. D – Running back David Johnson, 2nd, 4th

DID YOU KNOW?

1. The Cardinals made one of the worst trades in franchise history in 2011 when they acquired Philadelphia Eagles quarterback Kevin Kolb. Arizona shipped a 2nd round pick and defensive back Dominique Rodgers-Cromartie to the Eagles for the unproven signal-caller and then gave Kolb a five-year contract worth $64 million. The Cardinals released the ineffective quarterback in 2013, and he never played in another regular-season game.

2. The Cardinals fleeced the San Diego Chargers in a trade during the 1998 NFL Draft. The Chargers were desperate to draft Washington State quarterback Ryan Leaf and sent Arizona the 3rd pick, a 1999 1st round pick, a 2nd round pick, linebacker Patrick Sapp, and running back Eric Metcalf. However, the Cardinals' woeful scouting department failed to turn the three premium draft picks into productive players.

3. In their never-ending quest to find Carson Palmer's successor, the Cardinals sent a 7th round draft pick to the Philadelphia Eagles in 2015 for Matt Barkley. However, the former 4th round selection never stepped on the field for Arizona and was released the following season.

4. In need of a playmaker who could stretch defenses, the Cardinals acquired wide receiver Randal "Thrill" Hill from the Miami Dolphins in 1991 for a 1st round draft pick.

While the speedster managed only eight touchdowns in four seasons, he did catch 174 passes for 2,419 yards.

5. A contract dispute in New Orleans in 1991 led to the Cardinals acquiring cornerback Robert Massey for center Derek Kennard and a 5th round draft pick. Massey was selected to the Pro Bowl after a stellar 1992 campaign in which he returned three interceptions for touchdowns. Kennard won a starting position with the Saints but was lost for the season after three games due to a weight room accident.

6. A phone call from the Baltimore Ravens at the 2016 NFL Draft netted the Cardinals an extra 5th round pick. Arizona moved down from number 55 to 58 to allow the Ravens to select tight end Maxx Williams, and still got their preferred pass rusher, Marcus Golden. While Williams ended up playing for the Cardinals after four mediocre seasons in Baltimore, Golden led Arizona with 12.5 sacks during his rookie season. However, the Cardinals used the 5th round pick on a linebacker who never played a single game in the NFL.

7. With their eyes set on a young franchise quarterback, the Cardinals sent the number 15 pick, a 3rd round and a 5th round pick to the Oakland Raiders for the number 10 pick to select UCLA signal-caller Josh Rosen. The rookie threw 11 touchdowns and 14 interceptions as the Cardinals finished 3-13 to earn the top overall pick in the 2019 NFL Draft.

8. The Cardinals landed arguably the best wide receiver in the NFL in DeAndre Hopkins for a backup running back, a 2nd round draft pick, and a swap of 4th round choices. While the Houston Texans will get the services of often-injured running back David Johnson, this lopsided trade will undoubtedly raise expectations in Arizona in 2020.

9. The Kansas City Chiefs would probably like to forget about trading cornerback Marcus Cooper to the Cardinals in 2018 for a 7th round draft pick. The former Rutgers standout was named the starter early in the season and finished with a career-high 69 combined tackles and four interceptions in 13 starts. He was an alternate for the Pro Bowl and became a prized free agent who was too expensive for the Cardinals to re-sign.

10. With the addition of Kyler Murray as the top overall draft pick in 2019, the Cardinals dealt Josh Rosen to Miami for an unimpressive haul of two draft picks (2019 2nd round and 2020 5th round) for the 10th overall pick in 2018. Murray went on to win NFL Rookie of the Year honors, while Rosen served as a backup in Miami to veteran quarterback Ryan Fitzpatrick.

CHAPTER 13:

SUPER BOWL SPECIAL

QUIZ TIME!

1. How many NFL championships has the Cardinals franchise won since the team was founded in 1898?

   a. 0

   b. 1

   c. 2

   d. 3

2. Running back Elmer Angsman scored a pair of 70-yard touchdown runs to lead the Cardinals to the 1947 NFL title.

   a. True

   b. False

3. Which Hall of Fame running back scored the Cardinals' first touchdown in the 1947 NFL Championship Game?

   a. Ernie Nevers

   b. Jim Thorpe

c. Ollie Matson

d. Charley Trippi

4. Arizona was the second team in NFL history to reach the Super Bowl after winning only nine games during the regular season. What was the name of the first team with nine regular-season wins to advance to the Super Bowl?

   a. 1980 Dallas Cowboys

   b. 2001 Chicago Bears

   c. 1979 Los Angeles Rams

   d. 1991 New York Giants

5. The Cardinals boasted a trio of 1,000-yard wide receivers during their Super Bowl run in 2008. What was the name of these three receivers?

   a. Larry Fitzgerald, Anquan Boldin, David Boston

   b. Larry Fitzgerald, Anquan Boldin, Bryant Johnson

   c. Larry Fitzgerald, Anquan Boldin, Early Doucet

   d. Larry Fitzgerald, Anquan Boldin, Steve Breaston

6. The Cardinals reached Super Bowl XLIII with an inconsistent defense that allowed too many points. What was the defense's ranking during the regular season for points allowed?

   a. 17th

   b. 20th

   c. 28th

   d. 30th

7. Super Bowl XLIII was watched by 98.7 million viewers in

the United States, making it the most-watched Super Bowl in history at that time.

a. True

b. False

8. How much money did each Cardinals player receive for winning the 1947 NFL title?

a. $1,000

b. $1,132

c. $1,427

d. $1,653

9. Due to a slumping economy in the United States, what nickname was given to Super Bowl XLIII?

a. The Depression Bowl

b. The Slowdown Bowl

c. The Stagnation

d. The Recession Bowl

10. Which player scored the first points in Super Bowl XLIII?

a. Jeff Reed

b. Heath Miller

c. Ben Patrick

d. Gary Russell

11. The 1947 NFL Championship Game between the Cardinals and Eagles was the first NFL title game played after Christmas Day.

a. True

b. False

12. Which Arizona receiver caught a 64-yard touchdown pass with less than three minutes remaining in the game to give the Cardinals a three-point lead in Super Bowl XLIII?

    a. Anquan Boldin
    b. Bryant Johnson
    c. Larry Fitzgerald
    d. Steve Breaston

13. Arizona committed a whopping 11 penalties in Super Bowl XLIII. How many yards were the Cardinals penalized?

    a. 100
    b. 103
    c. 106
    d. 112

14. Which Arizona defensive tackle tallied three sacks in Super Bowl XLIII to tie the Super Bowl record set by Reggie White in Super Bowl XXXI?

    a. Calvin Pace
    b. Darnell Dockett
    c. Antonio Smith
    d. Calais Campbell

15. After winning the 1947 NFL championship, the Cardinals franchise did not win another playoff game for 51 years.

    a. True
    b. False

16. The Arizona Cardinals won the coin toss at Super Bowl XLIII to extend the NFC consecutive streak to how many Super Bowls?

   a. 10
   b. 11
   c. 12
   d. 13

17. Which Arizona coach led the franchise to their first NFL title game in over half a century?

   a. Joe Bugel
   b. Bruce Arians
   c. Ken Whisenhunt
   d. Gene Stallings

18. What was the attendance at the 1947 NFL Championship Game at Comiskey Park in Chicago?

   a. 30,759
   b. 26,412
   c. 34,806
   d. 29,144

19. Which Cardinals running back returned a punt for a 75-yard touchdown in the 1947 NFL Championship Game?

   a. Dub Jones
   b. Charley Trippi
   c. Pat Harder
   d. Ollie Matson

20. Super Bowl XLIII pitted two teams that had merged into a single team, "Card-Pitt," for the 1944 season due to a player shortage caused by World War II.

a. True
b. False

QUIZ ANSWERS

1. C – 2

2. A – True

3. D – Charley Trippi

4. C – 1979 Los Angeles Rams

5. D – Larry Fitzgerald, Anquan Boldin, Steve Breaston

6. C – 28th

7. A – True

8. B – $1,132

9. D – The Recession Bowl

10. A – Jeff Reed

11. B – False

12. C – Larry Fitzgerald

13. C – 106

14. B – Darnell Dockett

15. A – True

16. C – 12

17. C – Ken Whisenhunt

18. A – 30,759

19. B – Charley Trippi

20. A – True

DID YOU KNOW?

1. The Chicago Cardinals (9-3) entered the 1947 NFL Championship Game as 12-point favorites over the Philadelphia Eagles (8-4). The two teams had met in week 12 of the regular season with the Cardinals cruising to a lopsided 45-21 victory.

2. Following in the steps of the Seattle Seahawks, the Cardinals became only the second team in Super Bowl history to have both their city name and team nickname (Arizona Cardinals) painted in their end zone. In every other Super Bowl, teams have only featured their nicknames (Cardinals).

3. Due to a bad economy, Super Bowl XLIII was unlike any NFL championship game in recent memory. Besides low traffic both at restaurants and bars, *Sports Illustrated* and *Playboy* canceled their Super Bowl parties. Ticket scalpers also suffered as ticket prices plunged 40% from Super Bowl XLII.

4. Super Bowl XLIII was the third most-watched Super Bowl in history with an estimated total viewership of 151.6 million, including 98.7 million viewers in the United States. The big game was also the fourth most-watched U.S. television program of any kind.

5. For the first time in Super Bowl history, some viewers were treated to free porn during the live telecast of the

game. The analog feed of Comcast cable service was tampered with and 30 seconds of an adult cable television channel was broadcast to homes in Tucson and surrounding areas late in the fourth quarter immediately after a Cardinals touchdown. A man was later arrested in connection to the incident.

6. The 1947 NFL Championship Game was played on December 28, the latest the title matchup had ever been played. Comiskey Park hosted the NFL title game, and the temperature at kickoff was 29 degrees.

7. Although the United States economic downturn was evident at Super Bowl XLIII, a 30-second television commercial time slot cost up to $3 million for just the airtime. NBC, which aired the game, sold every advertising slot to earn $206 million in advertising sales.

8. Super Bowl XLIII had the unique distinction of having two of the NFL's oldest franchises battling for league supremacy. The Cardinals started as an independent amateur team in 1898 and were the oldest franchise in the NFC. The Steelers were formed in 1933 as the Pittsburgh Pirates and were the oldest franchise in the AFC.

9. Although the Steelers won the time of possession battle by having the ball 33 minutes and one second, the Cardinals dominated the offense statistics. Besides tallying a 23-20 advantage in first downs, Arizona also had more total yards (407-292) and passing yards (374-234).

10. The Steelers' victory in Super Bowl XLIII was marred by

riots in Pittsburgh after the title game. Several groups of rioters consisting mainly of college students caused heavy property damage celebrating the Steelers' sixth Super Bowl victory.

CONCLUSION

And there you have it! The greatest collection of Cardinals trivia to challenge your memory and knowledge of your favorite team. We trust you have enjoyed both the easy and the not-so-easy quiz questions, and that this book has enhanced your admiration for these gridiron stars.

While some of the trivia included in this book is for die-hard fans who have spent decades rooting for the Cards, there are also simple quiz questions for younger fanatics whose love affair with Arizona's favorite professional sports franchise is in its early stages.

Regardless of how well you fared taking these quizzes, the knowledge you will gain from this book will help you cement your credentials as an informed Cardinals fan. And you will also be prepared to educate others on the fascinating history of this up-and-coming franchise.

Did this book miss some key information that Cardinals supporters need to know? Perhaps, this book will inspire you to create your own quiz with details that have yet to be uncovered.

The future is bright for the new-look Arizona Cardinals and their loyal fans. Now is the time to jump on the bandwagon as the Big Red inches closer and closer to becoming a perennial playoff contender.